McPHEE GRIBBLE/PENGUIN BOOKS

THE MODERN GIRL'S GUIDE TO EVERYTHING

Kaz Cooke was bo
hasn't died yet. Be
elegance once, for
remain sketchy. A ╷   ⌐.⌐ ⌐⌐⌐⌐ school rounders
team and the private school co-educational treadmill, she
became a cub reporter in 1981 with the *Age*. She stayed
to write sharemarket reports (failing to wreck the economy
despite sincere effort), women's pages, general news and
Moslem Prayer Times. She is now the editor of the
Entertainment Guide, a freelance cartoonist and a
seasoned gym-dodger.

The Modern Girl's Guide To Everything

•starring HERMOINE the Modern Girl•

by

Kaz Cooke

McPHEE GRIBBLE/PENGUIN BOOKS

McPhee Gribble Publishers Pty Ltd
66 Cecil Street
Fitzroy, Victoria, 3065, Australia

Penguin Books Australia Ltd,
487 Maroondah Highway, P.O. Box 257
Ringwood, Victoria, 3134, Australia
Penguin Books Ltd,
Harmondsworth, Middlesex, England
Penguin Books,
40 West 23rd Street, New York, N.Y. 10010, U.S.A.
Penguin Books Canada Ltd,
2801 John Street, Markham, Ontario, Canada L3R 1B4
Penguin Books (N.Z.) Ltd,
182-190 Wairau Road, Auckland 10, New Zealand

First published by McPhee Gribble Publishers
in association with Penguin Books Australia 1986
Copyright © Karen Cooke, 1986

Typeset in Helvetica by Bookset, Melbourne
Made and printed in Australia by
The Dominion Press–Hedges & Bell
Designed by Meredith Parslow

National Library of Australia
Cataloguing-in-Publication data
Cooke, Kaz, 1962-
The Modern Girl's Guide to Everything
ISBN 0 14 010013 9
1. Young Women – Life skills guide. 1. Title.
646.7'0088042

Many of the cartoons in this book first appeared in the *Age* and the *Sydney Morning Herald* .

To my family and friends, who have had all their
best jokes stolen

CONTENTS

A DUBIOUS FOREWORD

Before I undertake the precarious business of introducing readers to this book allow me to establish my credentials. I am a forty-one year old married male and father of two children. My interest in Modern Girls, although warm and deep is definitely an academic, 'step fatherly' interest.* I am always ready to lend a guiding or comforting hand to any presentable Modern Girl who may be confused and troubled by this modern, unfathomable world. A quiet chat by the fire, a platonic walk in the moonlight to explain the mysteries of art and the universe, some homespun psychotherapy, advice on the choice of wines, a reassuring shoulder to cry on . . . my door has always been open to the open-minded Modern Girl.

This book provides for myself a very valuable insight into the fears and most interestingly, the weaknesses, of the Modern Girl. I have studied the manuscript at length in my den and taken certain notes so I can better understand the needs and secret longings of the present crop of youthful females and look forward immensely to putting this updated knowledge to practical application at the soonest possible opportunity.

I heartily recommend this work to all males facing mid-life crisis. If it can in some small way contribute to the bridging of the communication and generation gap between forty-ish males and open-minded young women, then Kaz will have performed a very generous service to mankind. On behalf of my generation and my gender I offer her my deepest and warmest congratulations.

Michael Leunig

*see 'Men to Steer Clear Of' p.7 .

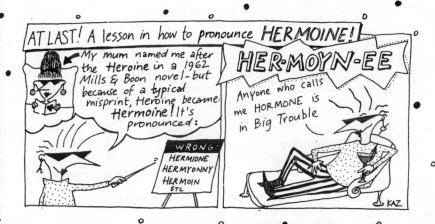

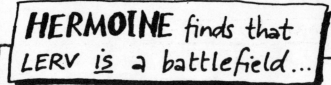

TRUE LERV AND ROMANCE

■ MR RIGHT, MR APPROXIMATE AND MR SLEAZE-SHMUCKO

I'm going to spoil the plot of every Mills and Boon novel ever written so you'll never have to read another one again. Boy meets girl. Girl blushes. They hate each other but girl feels strange attraction. Boy is horrible to girl. Girl gets into scrape. Boy saves girl. Boy marries girl.

Now in real life, this is not what happens. In real life it goes like this: Girl doesn't meet boy for ages. Girl finally meets boy, boy and girl fall in lerv. Boy is horrible to girl and girl cries. Girl kneecaps boy. Or: Boy meets girl, they fall in lerv and get married. Boy leaves girl for younger girl, girl kneecaps younger girl.

It's difficult to believe that anyone can find a lasting, wonderful

relationship in these times when Modern Girls outnumber Modern Boys by an estimated three zillion to one (statistics from the Modern Girl's World Health Organization, 1986). Of course if you are a girl seeking Ms Right it can be a lot easier. But for those of us still on the treadmill of heterosexuality, it's a case of still searching for the elusive Mr Right in the face of hardship beyond the call of the wild.

The much promised Sensitive New Man of the Eighties was almost extinct very soon after the species was identified. The ones that were roaming the streets were pounced on and dragged back into captivity by clever girls with interesting bone structure.

There should be a consumer's guide, or at least a kind of geiger-counter object we can skim over the lithe bodies of unsuspecting men. The object would emit a gentle warning signal if it's a **Mr Approximate**, send the needle off the end of the dial and give out a shrill scream if it's a **Mr Sleaze-Shmucko**. A glowing green light would herald (sigh) **Mr Right**. This would save an awful lot of tears, Telecom bills and time devoted to new hairstyles during an emotional crisis.

In the meantime we will all have to put up with trial, error and terror. Hang on to your dignity and your knickers until at least the third date, don't take any shit, and no matter HOW disastrous any situation you find yourself in, never, EVER sell your story to Willesee.

◼ MEN TO STEER CLEAR OF

Occasionally it is painfully and immediately obvious that a certain chap you are acquainted with ought to be given the heave-ho, the Big A, the flick-pass, the final word. This is usually when he is dribbling on your foot, or quoting a German philosopher's most obscure work in Norwegian, or telling you that you need a good screw.

7

Or asking you to iron his Y-fronts, or informing you that he's found a new girlfriend who is breathtakingly beautiful and far more interesting but he'd still like to see you on a physical basis, or when he's fallen asleep in the middle of the poem you wrote about him, and it's a haiku. Sometimes you can just tell a man isn't worth knowing, let alone developing a relationship that goes further than dealing him an icy stare whenever you meet.

There are several categories of rotters, not least among them the **Fake Feminist**. I really, really, hate fake feminists. These men are full of rhetoric about what a wonderful thing it is to be liberated from old-fashioned role models. They are particularly dangerous because they seem so wonderful, but don't mean a single word they say. Well, they might think they do, but it doesn't help when they are cruel to you, put you down in public, make snide remarks about things that are important to you, and insist that they are totally faithful right in the middle of a passionate affair with most of a suburban netball team.

Then there are **Men Who Simply Will Not Talk To You**. Oh they'll

talk to you about cricket scores and cloud formations and the funny stuff that collects in the bottom of trouser cuffs and their habit of shooting out street lights on full moons, but they won't converse with you on anything more important, like love and politics and why you don't look good in yellow.

The **Irretrievably Flippant Chap** is another no-no. He makes a habit of turning every situation into a bad pun, even your latest bout of cystitis and the time your granny fell out of the apricot tree. He refuses to take anything seriously, especially you. He never, but never turns up on time and laughs when you broach the subject. 'Oh, I was out,' he'll say airily. He thinks your job is a huge joke and your latest painting was 'nice enough'. He has deep personal scars on his psyche and ought to be left alone.

Conversely, the **Serious Types** can be much, much worse. At least you'll get the odd giggle out of Mr Flippant. You'll know when you've hit a serious type when he wants to discuss the decline of the dollar: in the bath. He'll ask you to read articles on foreign debt,

9

the phenomenon of insurance premiums and the latest scientific research into spleen malfunctions and blood circulation in the people of Northern Quambatook. He will require a short verbal review of everything to be reported at your next dinner date.

He thinks red shoes, comedy and watching rock videos in bed with chocolate are a waste of time and money. His favourite night out is attending a seminar on Personal Goals and Marketing Techniques in Today's Busy World for People Who Matter in the Scheme of Things Because They Have Developed Inner Confidence And A Jolly Firm Handshake Indeed.

The list is almost endless, but the field of men to avoid can be basically narrowed to:

Barflies, all married men, sportsmen (can't bonk on Friday nights), politicians, all married men, farmers (if you get hayfever), schoolboys (if you abhor jail), men who belong to male feminist groups which meet on his night to do the dishes, men who won't let you cut your hair, junkies, manic depressives, bondage freaks

(unless you like it), misogynists, all married men, men who don't like you going out with the girls, men who can talk for hours about tennis, men who wear menacing shirts and polyester moustaches, men who blow their nose in the shower, journalists.

FIRST DATES

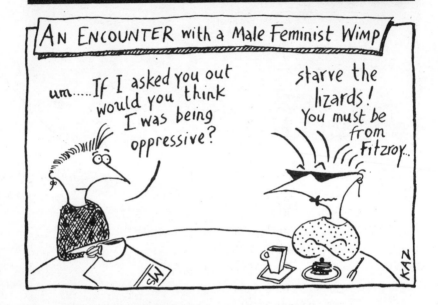

An Encounter with a Male Feminist Wimp

um......If I asked you out would you think I was being oppressive?

starve the lizards! You must be from Fitzroy...

■ TO BONK OR NOT TO BONK

Dinner and a movie is perfectly adequate. For heaven's sake don't cook for the man until at least two weeks after making his acquaintance. Apart from the inevitable frazzle you'll be in when the warm salad with French fennel curdles and the cat eats the sauce and throws up inelegantly on your new red suede shoes, cooking so early will set an ugly precedent. OK, so you've been to dinner and had a pleasant enough time and managed to avoid too many awkward silences that you both rushed to fill at the same time and discovered that he doesn't eat with his mouth open or pat

waitresses. You split the bill, or the richest person pays by prior arrangement (no ropes attached). The movie was passable except for the embarrassing, preceding short film about sexually transmitted diseases, and your stomach only rumbled imperceptibly during the noisy massacre scenes. You emerge on the street. BUT NOW WHAT? Consider the possibilities:

- He kisses you on the cheek/shakes your hand (it has been known)/slaps you athletically on the back and you go your separate ways.

- You go for a drink, which only prolongs the agony.

- You go to his place or your place for coffee/port/to watch all night rock videos, which brings up the question: will you spend the night together?

Recommended timeframe for this sort of behaviour is either ten minutes after meeting him, or on the third date. Anything else would be unbecoming. But it's excruciating just getting around to asking. Especially if he's shy. And let's face it, you're unlikely to

13

be seeing a boy known for flying rugby tackles and lustful shouts as a method of foreplay. And if you are, you would have been bonking ten minutes after meeting him. So here are some foolproof methods of getting him into bed and conversely, some surefire ways of making sure you don't get anywhere near it.

■ IF YOU WANT HIM TO STAY

Let his tyres down; ask him if he's on the pill; ask him 'would you help me move this?' indicating the couch, and move it in front of the door; say 'I thought I'd stay here tonight, how about you?' (not to be used at his place); kiss him a lot until his mind is full of nothing but sex, sex, sex and you; refrain from tweaking him encouragingly on the penis.

Hermoine the Modern Girl at the Sensitive New Man Library...

I'd like to borrow an artist please

Sorry, they're all out. Have a poet...

Two weeks of bliss!

Let me wash the dishes. Do you have enough personal space? etc, etc

JUSTIN

■ IF YOU DON'T WANT TO SLEEP WITH HIM

Ask him to drive to an all-night shop for two packets of tampons; set off a beeper and exclaim ruefully, 'Gosh-darn, an emergency.

Must fly'; regale him with a witty anecdote about your last visit to the herpes clinic; go into the toilet, climb out the window and run (not to be used at your place); mention your quaint but disconcerting habit of trying to throttle people in your sleep; play Loretta Lynn's version of 'Stand By Your Man' and talk about babies.

ACTUAL HONEST TO GOD NO GETTING AROUND IT NITTY GRITTY SEX

Nothing to be scared of really. The first time usually is awful. Not just THE first time, but often the first time with anyone new. Not surprisingly – after all, the area between his neck and ankles is probably totally unfamiliar territory unless you met him at a male strip joint and, honey, you shouldn't have been there in the first place. And likewise, he's probably worrying about what YOU want. All that pounding heartbeat isn't just unbridled passion, some of it is sheer terror.

You'll just have to tell him what you like, although this may be difficult on the first occasion unless you are exceptionally bold. ('Hi Charles, I'm Felicia and I like slow cunnilingus and doing it standing up in the shower.') If you're too scared to talk about sex, you may need to get a little drunk or a little stoned before you pluck up the courage. If you're too sensible for that, turn the light off, then at least he can't see you blushing.

Mostly all the usual sex stuff is quite satisfactory in the early stages: lots of kissing, touching, hours of playing around and good old-fashioned bonking. At this heady stage you probably can't get enough of each other. And PLEASE try not to think about whether he'll like your tits or whether you have too much cellulite. He'd hardly be nibbling on your left ear and murmuring all sorts of delicious, wicked things if he found you vile and untouchable, would he?

It's later in the The Relationship, when you can't decide whether to go ten-pin bowling or take each other's clothes off with your teeth and go to bed with strawberries and champagne, that you are going to run into serious trouble.

You're going to have to leave town (the best way to break up with someone) or Revive Things. Revive things? Yup. Put in a little work. Do it in the Botanical Gardens (unless you're likely to get arrested), go away for a dirty weekend, read filthy literature, do it when you wake up in the middle of the night, wear suspenders, make him wear suspenders (how did this get in here?), dip yourself in dark chocolate, seduce him, drive him crazy. If he's obviously not interested and prefers to watch Madonna videos, THEN leave town.

■ A FEW IMPERATIVES ABOUT SEX

- Make time for it, even if it's two pm on a Saturday.
- Ensure your partner knows where your clitoris is and avails himself freely of this information.
- Only do it with people you really, really like. Any other reason is simply bullshit and not worth hearing about.
- Don't do it to try and get an old boyfriend back.

- Don't be tacky. If a man likes black satin sheets and wants to call you 'Mummy' or 'Princess', that's a good reason to dump him, not to oblige.

- Always tell the truth. If it lasted two minutes and most of that was friction, say so gently and make a suggestion or three. Do not, under any circumstances, leave a copy of *The Joy of Sex* anonymously under his pillow. If necessary, delicately remind him that girls like orgasms, too. If he turns on the footy replay when you mention oral sex for girls, you'll know it's time to hit the road.

One thing about sex that's hard to avoid is that you're going to come into contact with a penis. No, don't make a face like that. You may as well get used to it, even if you didn't see one until you were fifteen and that was in a science textbook. A word of advice: know your subject. Although I am not going to go into details here, suffice to say the object in question seems to respond to almost any attention at all as long as it involves a minimum of brute force and a minimum of pathetic, barely felt pats. Find a happy medium and you'll make someone more than medium happy. (NEVER bite.)

■ CONTRACEPTION IS BORING

Actually contraception is worse than boring. It is just plain, unavoidably, mind-numbingly, infuriatingly tedious. There you are thinking all kinds of warm happy thoughts about bonking and having someone blow in your ear and suddenly a full-color picture of a pram bursts, unannounced, into your brain. Babies! Yuk! (Unless you really want one, in which case, skip the contraception section for a few weeks.)

There's only one thing worse than getting your period, and that's not getting your period. Pregnancy scares are definitely not boring, they are scary and lead us to consider difficult questions, such as, 'If I decide to have an abortion will Right To Life demonstrators burst into the foyer of the hospital and make me feel even more miserable?' So let's have a look at the various contraceptive methods now available. I don't know what these scientists have

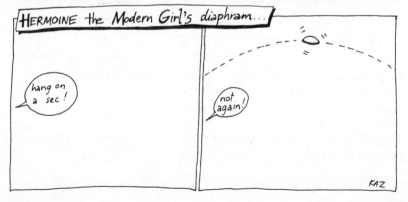

been DOING all these years, because they certainly haven't found a cure for too many unwanted pregnancies. Too busy with rats and bombs, that's their trouble.

The Rhythm Method: Forget it. There's a true story about a Catholic couple who circled the 'safe' days in each month on their complimentary Arnott's Biscuits calendar (the one with the Rosella on it). Unfortunately, every time the husband felt a trifle frisky, he'd tear the calendar off the wall yelling: 'No bloody parrot is going to tell me when I can have relations!' In the end he did have many relations, not least among them his ten children. I rest my case.

Condoms: Protection against icky diseases. Liable to go inside out at the slightest provocation. You could practise on a banana, but lock the door to avoid embarrassing scenes. Check for runs and ladders.

Diaphragm: A contentious issue. Some girls swear by it and carry it everywhere, just in case. They have hopeful eyes. Some even claim to have mastered the crochet-hook-like inserter especially for manoeuvres with a 7.8 degree of difficulty. Come to think of it, if iceskating is accepted, I don't see why diaphragm insertion can't be an Olympic sport. Many girls tend to find that the object is impossibly single-minded about springing out of girlish hands and zinging across the room, merrily gathering momentum and fluff. Unfortunately, diaphragms are the best and safest contraception for Modern Girls. It's enough to make you mega-petulant.

The Pill: Seems deceptively easy, if you can remember to take it. Prone to side effects.

IUD: Last resort. Only if your doctor REALLY recommends it and you really trust your doctor, and you have really regular check-ups and it doesn't make your period go really beserk so you have to carry a packing case full of tampons everywhere you go.

Vasectomy: Great, but often accompanied by a married man (*see* Men To Steer Clear Of).

Sponges, Douches, Coitus Interruptus, Hoping, Crossing Fingers: all about the same rate of success.

HERMOINE and HOW to Have A Good Cry:

Props: One HUGE box of tissues, telephone. Repeat all problems to yourself at LEAST twice.

Do not allow anyone to cheer you up until you're good & ready. Then... CUT LOOSE!

All men are Creeps... I'm too fat... the budgie died of mange etc etc

WACKO!

LIFE: HUG IT FURTIVELY

LENTIL dacquiri

KAZ

■ HEARTBREAK: GETTING OVER IT

There is no section in this book about getting into heartbreak for obvious reasons. That's easy. Ah, yes, skirmishes of the heart. Some despicable cad has taken your heart, thrown it in the blender and fed it to the chooks. He's dumped you cold and gone off with some mindless newt with Cheekbones and a Georges charge-account.

You've cried until your face looks like it's done ten rounds with stinging nettles, your nose is unrecognizable (not that you liked it in the first place. Go on: wallow in misery) and your chest hurts. Your mascara is heading steadily south, causing you to resemble nothing so much as an inconsolable giant panda.

Stop it. Take a look at yourself. No, not in the mirror, I mean metaphorically. Who does he think he is, anyway, leaving a certified darling like you? After all you've done (and not done, like eating chocolates in bed). Your friends love you, so why shouldn't he?

Just a minute, did someone say FRIENDS? Yeah, remember them? All right it's time to kick arse on this heartbreak business. Rally those who love you best. Tell EVERYONE what a shit he is. Have a haircut. Buy a new outfit. Gain five pounds or lose five pounds, whatever will make you happier. Go to the gym, swim, or throw yourself into something else, as long as it isn't straight into the arms of someone else. After all, if you'd got food poisoning from an African artichoke, you wouldn't eat another one the next day.

Go out with the girls; go to the footy with your little brother and barrack with abandon, pretending that the umpire is your ex. Don't just put on a brave front, *be* brave. You might still think about him every day, but that's just a bad habit. Time heals nearly everything, except nuclear war and beetroot stains.

If revenge is called for, put prawns in his hub caps. He'll have something to remind him what a stinker he is for quite some time until he works out where the all-pervading odour is coming from. Or break into his house, ring the Amsterdam automatic weather report and leave the phone off the hook. Give him the polite cold shoulder. If he speaks to you, regard him somewhat absent-mindedly as if you're almost positive you have met this person somewhere before.

Don't read Barbara Cartland novels. Do not become a groupie. Don't even think about tattoos. Who needs a man as an accessory? You're all right, sister, all by yourself, believe it. And if you don't believe it, go put 'Respect' by Aretha Franklin on the turntable.

FASHION

Hermoine The Modern Girl's **FASHION TIPS**

No	No	Yes	Oh Yes
Anything in lime Crimplene	Soup Stains	Dancing Shoes	Edible Earrings

A wardrobe full of old ra-ra skirts, purple paisley, nylon sarongs, hobble skirts and platform thongs testify to your essentially fickle taste. You probably have approximately seven thousand items of apparel (as they say in the glossy magazines. One does not *wear* clothes, one tells a fashion story, drapes, or generally slips into something expensive) but still we murmur sadly, 'Oh, what am I going to wear?' at the drop of a you know what.

And going shopping doesn't help much. Either you're faced with chainstore hideousness (buy that dress, and you'll look like one hundred thousand other girls this summer and some of them will look better in it) or worse, be confronted with New Designers. New designers do not have shops. They have spaces, where you can EXPERIENCE their clothes.

The New Designers describe their clothes something like this: assymetrical sex couture, a post post-punk myriad of organza and metal alloy junk-funk look with a less-is-more, elegant yet street story featuring unpretentious latex rubber trapdoors for that air of quiet reserve with a Tex-Mex cowgirl ruched tulle crimson bridal look with thigh boots.

This is all very well if you spend your day mincing down a catwalk with a studious sneer and half a kilo of eyeliner on your face. Few Modern Girls fit this category. So we end up desperately hurling ourselves at Portmans or Sportsgirl and buying something mass-produced which we all know we can ACCESSORIZE to make it practically unrecognizable because everyone is so knocked out by our witty scarf or battery operated earrings they don't even notice the rest. Ha.

■ WHAT EVERY GIRL NEEDS AS A BASIC WARDROBE

Five pairs of black tights, some with fetching ladders; one LBD

You can tell a lot about a Modern Girl by what's in her Glomesh bag...

spare shades — dead lipstick — groovy magazine — spanner — dole cheque — cocktail umbrella — fluff — gel — $2.60

(Little Black Dress); red shoes; loud gymboots; jeans; flannelette shirt; large jumper of dubious origins; hatpin for self defence; one organdy-silk dreamy pink ballgown that used to belong to Grace Kelly found in the Ulladulla op-shop which fits perfectly (optional); Speedos; 473 pairs of cotton undies with questionable elastic; 740 earrings (some in pairs), mostly large and tacky; purple socks; and a becoming sun-hat.

Hermoine gets a Make-Over, just like in The Magazines!

before — URRGH

during

after — Yeah, I'm a new woman. I used to be a right berk but now that's all changed etc etc etc

■ BOUTIQUE SALES ASSISTANTS

A word of advice about boutique sales assistants. This breed apart is made up of two types. Those on commission and those on wages. It will be difficult to find a sales assistant on wages because he or she will be chatting to a friend on the phone or doing their fingernails.

The assistant who gets a commission on sales (say, ten per cent) will follow you about like a Blue Heeler, burst into the change room with no provocation to suggest another three outfits you would look DIVINE in. Not only that, but an assistant on commission will tell you that a skin-tight lime polyester pant-suit with flares and no waist is 'flattering'. Indeed, 'absolutely you'.

Pay no attention. Take as long as you like, view everything from all angles, walk around in it, sit down before you decide. After all, you're going to be the one who sees this particularly divine hot-pink-shorts-and-matching-frilly-top ensemble in your wardrobe for the next few years.

■ SWIMWEAR

If the department stores had any sense and a nose for a real profit, they'd put rose-coloured lighting in swimwear changerooms. It's spring and you peel off your jeans and gymboots to try on a size 10, sleek, natty little patterned one-piece with no straps. 10,000 watts of fluorescent lights pound relentlessly onto your well-upholstered form, showing every curve, every dimple, every goddamned mohair stocking and winter tummy. Suddenly in a violent temper, you despair of ever revealing yourself at Bondi or South Melbourne in anything less than a canvas caftan, throw the bathers back at a snarling sales assistant (on commission), dismiss the bikini racks with a wry grimace, and stride off to the nearest sensible sports store for Speedos. Which is what you should have done in the first place: after all, this happened last year, remember?

■ FASHION GLOSSARY

Stylish = black
Elaborate = downright absurd
Exclusive = astonishingly expensive
Stark and simple = bearing a remarkable resemblance to a wheat sack
Funky = worn by keyboard players in obscure bands
Cheeky = almost see-through
Delicate = utterly see-through
Wearable = will not cut off circulation
Bold = purple and green eyeshadow
Arresting = purple and green lipstick
Exotic = to be worn with red lipstick and a sulk
Erotic = lingerie
Crisp = you could cut yourself on the pleats
White = attracts the dirt
Slinky = will fall off if you move
Complete fashion story = remembering to put knickers on
Cluttered = it takes three hours to dress and four hours to untangle
Feminine = prone to hideous frills
With a name label = double the cost of similar outfit elsewhere
Tailored = with lapels
Understated = extremely dull
Androgenous = trousers
Witty = only good for fancy dress parties
One size fits all = enormous
Oversized = positively elephantine

■ GREAT HAIRDRESSING DISASTERS

For the purposes of this sorrowful exercise we'll assume the hairdresser is a male.

You sidle into the hairdressing salon, suddenly bereft of former convictions to do something drastic. The hairdresser flashes you a cheesy grin, a what-are-you-doing-in-a-place-like-this-cupcake grin, the likes of which you have come to expect from men at parties wearing polyester shirts and a menacing moustache. The kind of smile to dim the MCG lights on a moonless night. 'Selina!' he intones with great warmth. Your name is not Selina. A frown crosses his artistic features. He was sure Selina was booked in at 4.30 but he'll fit you in, he assures you. This leaves him 3.8 minutes to give you a cut, style, root perm, highlights and a blow wave.

Preliminaries dispatched, and an apprentice sent to make you weak instant coffee, you are propelled to a chair into the hands of another apprentice whom you suspect nurtures ambitions to be a fire fighter with a speciality in wide-beam hose-nozzles, judging by the liberal deluge she deals you with the spray-hose thingie.

By the time you leave the chair fitted with patented extras especially designed to cause permanent neck problems, and frequently used by manic dentists (has anyone ever actually snapped their vertebrae while being shampooed, I wonder?) you look like you've been caught in a tropical storm. Your hair, but not the rest of you, dries while you read a 1978 copy of *Cosmopolitan* and the hairdresser is attending to Selina, a rather gorgeous sort with television connections. OK, now it's your big moment: The Chat. 'What would you like?' says the hairdresser. At this particular moment you'd like to hurl yourself from the chair and run screaming to the nearest coffee shop. All thoughts of daring yet flattering styles flee your tortured mind. 'Just a trim thanks,' you mumble with a brave, yet watery smile. Oh, no you don't, thinks the hairdresser.

'Dahling,' he says, with an indulgent chuckle. 'I don't DO trims. I mean, you come to an expert, you can't insult him like that. You wouldn't ask Paul Keating to draw up the tuck shop budget, would you? I think I should remind you that you are dangerously close to toying with my artistic credibility, my reason for being – hair is my life, I dream about it constantly.'

There is a short, tearful spell before the man recovers his composure. 'I recommend a shave here, and here,' he says, (indicating an area dangerously close to the ears). 'Short HERE (the back) and long here (indicating the rest) with black underneath at the back, and a Rampant Jaffa rinse – very subtle – through the top. Trust me.'

The hairdresser shows you a picture of this hairstyle on a model who would look good BALD for heaven's sake, and you go into a sort of coma. God I hate The Chat.

The weapons are produced. Pinking shears, a wide tooth comb (union approved) a bucket of gel, a gale-force hairdryer and some combs that don't seem to have any space between the teeth – yours are much the same, gritted as they are.

I feel we should stop the narrative here, because describing your new haircut as something Phyllis Diller would reject as unbecoming will just increase the likelihood of tears long before bedtime, much locking of oneself in the bathroom, bomb threats, international legal suits and ugly recriminations all round.

'What can be done about this?' I hear you ask plaintively.

Firstly, NEVER recommend a hairdresser to a friend, because she will hold you responsible for the dire consequences, and with guilt about world starvation and the arms race, who needs the extra burden?

Secondly, find yourself a tame hairdresser who has never heard of the term 'artistic credibility' unless they read it by accident.

Be nice to your hairdresser. Be extremely nice to your hairdresser. Tell them exactly what you want. Conversely, if you prefer to put your tresses in the scissors of the gods and hope for the best, try not to complain afterwards. After all, saying 'Do what you want' is asking for some extraordinary responses.

Face up to your responsibilities, or go and live in another state for a while. Dye it if you want, but not black if you're blonde. And don't try to get a job in an advertising agency if you dye it a vivacious green. In fact, don't try to get a job at an advertising agency under any circumstances. Modern Girls must have SOME dignity in their lives.

HEALTH

HERMOINE the Modern Girl..and a New Year!

I'm going to give up daiquiris, boys, staying up late and choccy biscuits

until at least three o'clock...

KAZ

Health is a good thing to have, and you don't need to have jelly-bean coloured lurex aerobics leotards. Essentially, if you are sick, you should see a doctor.

Despite the obvious, many people don't. Instead, they worry themselves even sicker, or write to *Cleo* or *Dolly*, with questions such as 'I have a vaginal discharge the consistency of steak diane and a rash over fifty per cent of my body' or 'I have a lump in my breast, what should I do?' or 'I have been having headaches for ten years and my tinea is reaching epic proportions.'

The answer to all these complaints is: go and see a doctor, for heaven's sake. Not just any doctor. Choosing a doctor is a crucial decision in any woman's life. At the slightest hint that you are getting short-shrift, not being told the truth, or are being treated in a way which suggests to you that the doctor assumes that you failed kindergarten finger-painting: find another doctor.

Going to the doctor is a service that you are paying for. Let's face it, your consultations could be the downpayment on the bumper bar of the next Porsche, so shop around, or get a friend to recommend someone to you.

Going to a doctor can be an unpleasant experience: in an ideal world the only contact we have with stirrups ought to be watching Princess Anne in an equestrian event, but the harsh reality is that every six months or so we should go and have a check-up for cervical cancer, outrageous blood pressure, general mental instability, knock knees, breast cancer, and bad breath.

It's a bit of a chore, but it's better than finding out too late that your complaint could have been dealt with a lot earlier in the piece. While all the gynaecological stuff is going on down there, look at the ceiling and think of your favourite film star, plan your shopping list, or run over the reasons why you will never wear flared satin trousers, it won't take long. If your doctor doesn't warm the instruments used in these circumstances, threaten to put ice down his or her back.

Of course health isn't necessarily just the absence of illness. (Someone incredibly sensible once said that.) To be healthier, you have to do things like get enough vitamins, avoid situations likely to unhinge you mentally, keep reasonably fit, eat spinach and other green things (lime junket is optional), stave off cravings to be an alcoholic or drug dependent zombie, have a shot to immunize you against German measles and eat less than two blocks of chocolate per day over a yearly average.

JUNK FOOD TRAINING: Hermoine as a baby

shake, rattle and roll

KAZ

■ DIET AND EXERCISE

Don't come snivelling around this section looking for a magic answer. If there was a magic answer we could finally get rid of those horrible TV ads for slimming courses. 'I lost twenty-five stone in three weeks, Joan, and my husband is so happy,' they say, forgetting to add that the miracle programme seems to have had some kind of alarming effect on their brain cells and has caused them to take on the speech patterns of one of the androids in the 1952 classic 'Mars Takes Over The Prom Night With Ray Guns'.

There is a trillion-zillion-squillion dollar industry based around the fact that women cannot stick to diets. Well, why the hell should they? There's never any chocolate in them for a start. Not only that, but a person on a diet is constantly denying herself, which is definitely not something to be encouraged.

The real answer to all this nonsense is not really that one ought to be thinner, just that one ought to be FITTER. Full of beans. Raring to

go. Hotter than a pepper sprout. Able to sprint after trains without collapsing with serious blue tinges to the gills.

The interesting thing about being fit, is that it has a serious side-effect: no excess weight. Isn't that neat? So either accept your more well-upholstered image or, if you want to be thinner, the best thing to do is to get fit.

There are several ways to do this including aerobics, tennis, sixty-seven sit-ups every day at precisely seven am, abseiling, running, swimming and going to the gym. Hockey is effective, but sometimes fatal. The intended insult 'playing like a girl' was probably coined by a wimpy eighteen stone Rugby League player who has never witnessed a Schoolgirl Horror Bloodbath Shock Hockey Match. The best forms of exercise are bonking and dancing.

■ DRUGS

That little chappie from the Vice Squad detailed to read this book can breathe more easily: this book will not recommend wholesale drug-taking and will be extremely Responsible About The Whole Subject. But while you're reading this, sergeant, please pass on a request to your colleagues to go easy on the small-time dope smokers and send a few heavies around to pick up the heroin dealers. (There, that got rid of the police readers. They've heard that plea often enough now to send them to sleep every time, especially in New South Wales.)

For the rest, the main drugs we will come into contact with are alcohol, cigarettes, chocolate, romance, and daytime television, which are all extremely seductive, addictive and very, very dangerous. All should be treated with care and shunned when appropriate. If you are taking too much of any of these things – and in the case of cigarettes, that's more than half a day (fags, not packets) – stop it or seek professional help. Especially alcohol,

which makes things look all right on the night, but you never respect yourself in the morning.

Right, that's got rid of all the parents reading this far, so it's time to give you Hermoine the Modern Girl's recipe for the perfect cocktail:

Find a dark corner of a respectable cocktail dispensing establishment with clean tables and cute waiters – sorry, that's sexist – waiters you can relate to in a deep and lasting personal sense, and order a Midori Sour: equal parts Midori which is a bright green melon liqueur (you need more greens in your diet, remember?), Cointreau, lemon juice, and frivolity.

Drink and pay for more than one of these and you will be broke, but you won't care. Besides, as a bonus you usually get a little paper umbrella and a lemon twist and a machismo cherry, sorry, maraschino cherry on a darling little toothpick that you will discard into the ashtray along with the hospital-issue bendy straw. Midori Sours tend to make one's words, and worlds, all blend together in the giant cocktail shaker of life.

■ GIVING UP SMOKING

There is no doubt that giving up smoking is A Good Idea. It must also be said that it is as hard as finding Mr Right and a better excuse than pre-menstrual tension for turning into an impossibly grumpy, homicidal maniac. It makes no difference that The Blonde With The Bone Structure in the menthol cigarette ads probably has the beginnings of a fetching case of lung cancer. No matter that she smells like a week-old ashtray. So what if her teeth have been given a couple of coats of Liquid Paper to cover the nicotine stains.

You want a cigarette. Now. And you might maim in order to get one. Or scrabble through tea leaves and ancient yoghurt in the bin to find a butt. Or stroll through a cyclone for a drag on an unfiltered Gitane. The tobacco companies point out that they have a perfectly legal right to maintain their huge profits by selling Modern Girls the means to a grisly end. It's a slow and elegant death as long as it's done off-camera. You could always hurl yourself off the bridge, it's easier than giving up smoking. Got a match?

■ PMT

Ever since a few British women pleaded Pre-Menstrual Tension (PMT) as a defence in murder cases, a lot of men look really scared when you tell them you have stomach cramps*. They secretly fear that inside every woman is a bizarre serial killer ready to fly off the handle at the slightest provocation for about two days a month.

*The only time you're likely to get off a murder charge with a defence of PMT is if a man tells you that shaving once a day is worse than getting your period once a month. Now *that's* grounds for murder.

Reality is rather different. Women who suffer (and some really suffer) from PMT are far less likely to fling themselves upon someone calling for a serrated-edge axe than they are to mope around the house, clutch at their middle region, burst into tears, feel tired and grumpy and start gnawing at the legs of tables out of sheer hunger and new-found perversity.

Some women feel no ill-effects at all. These jolly, hearty, despicable souls never brought notes from home during sport days, and have never experienced the very real sensation that there is a family of hyperactive bandicoots running around doing terrible things to their insides. 'PMT?' they exclaim, 'never understood what all the fuss is about, frankly. Anyone for rock-climbing?'

Then there are others who can hardly bring themselves to crawl out of bed on 'bad days', who bravely drag themselves about, stopping only to swoon, lie down again, fill another hot water bottle, or make themselves another cup of comfrey tea. Tablets are available from the health food shop on the shelf between desiccated seaweed and beancurd soya-milk pavlova; or at the chemist between the facial

HERMOINE gets P.M.T at a night class in CHEMISTRY.

now students, be careful of your equipment

Sorry sir, I accidentally split the atom

massager with vibrating action conveniently shaped like a penis, and the exfoliating wire mitts for leg hairs. If this is what life has come to, no wonder PMT is so depressing.

Although you may have heard that all periods go for five days each month with a break of twenty-eight days in between, some Modern Girls have clocked up regular cycles lasting forty days in between menstruating (lucky sods) or sixteen days (there ought to be a medal).

CULTURE

There's not a lot one can say on this subject. One girl's Culture is another's existentialist angst and if you think that's confusing, you should hear some film theorists talk. Jabbering endlessly about thematic semiology and the significance of the word 'and' in the context of communication, it's enough to make your head swim.

Various aspects of Culture are best enjoyed alone, like reading romance novels in a bubble bath or sitting in the back row of a sad movie with a family box of tissues. It is possible to thoroughly enjoy a film like 'Raiders Of The Lost Ark', despite the lack of non-sexist Modern Girl role models, although this is largely due to the time spent perving at Harrison Ford. Art Galleries can be a soothing experience, especially when you have a headache. Unless it is an

exhibition by an artist during her Completely Bonkers Pre-Menstrual Tension Nervous Breakdown Blue Period, which will give you a headache.

There is much to be said for Culture when it involves a decent live theatre performance or a jolly good sing along but Culture can also cause hideous injuries, especially to the ears at teeny-bopper concerts and to the boredom threshhold during Sylvester Stallone films.

■ WHEN TO GET UP AND WHEN TO GET DOWN

Getting up is to be avoided for as long as possible, unless you are committed to a complicated array of hideous, pre-dawn weight-lifting. Eleven in the morning is a good time to get up and three in the afternoon is even better, especially if the previous evening is only vaguely recalled as a pleasant haze of daiquiris and dancing.

Which brings us to when to get down which is also known as dancing – and the answer is anytime, but keep in mind that it will probably be frowned upon at job interviews, during classical music recitals and while in bed with a new boyfriend. If the new boyfriend doesn't mind, kidnap him immediately: he is a gem.

■ STICKY SITUATIONS: BEING HASSLED OR BORED AT A PARTY

You know the scene, some drongo in a polyester shirt and a loud moustache has you pinned against the wall and is talking about insurance, or his wife, or what it's like to do it on a waterbed. You really, really don't need this, and besides, there's your friend Clarissa over there looking lonely. Use soft options on those who are merely dull and get out the big guns for the leery leches.

- Hiss: 'You are disgusting. Remove yourself from my presence or I shall remove myself from yours.' This is surprisingly effective.

- In the case of men who only understand words of one syllable, 'Piss Off' will do nicely.

- Don't make a scene unless you know a back way out, your nearby friends are well-muscled, or it looks like it could be fun.
- Talk about hydroponics.
- Spit.
- Spill hot coffee in his lap (especially at dinner

parties where under-table sexual harassment has ensued) and apologize with a reptilian smile.

- Put your hand over your mouth and say in muffled tones 'I think I'm going to be sick'.

- Go off to get another drink. If your drink is full, pour it on his foot.

HERMOINE...and Girls' Talk

You think you've been left on the shelf?

Yeah, and my shelf-life is limited.

You're going to give up looking for Mr Right?!!...

Let's just say I have an "amuse-by" date

■ GOSSIP

Delicious, isn't it? Don't believe anyone who says they don't. It's like masturbation: irresistible. But make sure you can keep a secret and your friends know it.

If you find out your girlfriend's boyfriend is bonking someone else, ALWAYS tell her. She might crumple up like a well-Ajaxed Wettex at first but it is her right to know (wouldn't you feel the same?). You should only tell, of course, if you have substantial evidence – not a scrap of overheard conversation that went something like: 'Gerald . . . Felicia . . . bo . . . I . . . air . . . was no . . . oh.' This could mean:

'Gerald and Felicia have been bonking like there was no tomorrow,' but it could mean: 'Gerald told Felicia she was so boring and stupid, it was fair to say she was no Plato.'

If you have to tell your girlfriend something like this, take her out and get her drunk on cocktails if you can afford it, cheap plonk if you can't (but only let her do this for one night). Steer the conversation along the lines of 'shits we have known' and make elaborate plans for his imaginary demise. While we're on the subject, NEVER bonk a girlfriend's boy. It isn't worth it. Girlfriends last forever if they're good ones. Even good boys often don't.

WORK

Almost everyone who works tries to find ways to do less of it, and almost everyone who is unemployed tries to get some work. To be employed is to be inundated by new concepts such as tax, overtime, flexitime, bad times, no time for anything else, lunch breaks, superiors, endlessly ringing telephones, worker's compensation, and especially pay day.

To be unemployed is to be smartly introduced to closely inspecting the odd-sock rack at the laundromat, shoplifting the wrong size knickers at the supermarket, furtively ferreting down the back of friend's couches for loose change, chopping up the kitchen table for firewood, and ordering a small lemonade when you really want a Crazy Wacko Jumbo Rocket Fuel Cocktail in a coconut shell with three paper umbrellas and a star-shaped piece of imported fresh pineapple on top.

Not to mention no money, no fun, no rent, no dice, no way, no situations vacant, noble stiff upper lips and specifically, dole day. All in all it is better to be employed, unless you are independently wealthy, which has its own problems because probably everyone secretly hates you.

Working means getting up in the morning (unless you are a shift worker) even when it is absolutely freezing or a perfect beach day. It means not wearing orange parachute pants and a gold lame bikini top with a stuffed parrot on one shoulder. It means not being able to say 'Stuff this up your bum and rotate, you sleazebucket' to your boss. And it means learning to despise inanimate objects, like telephones, desks, computers and members of the paying public.

There are other drawbacks to being employed, such as being injured. This happens to your feelings all the time, but sometimes it happens to your body. One of the most common work injuries for Modern Girls is RSI: repetitive strain injury. It sounds like something you get listening to the yearly pep talk from the accounts department, but it is more serious even than that.

It means that if you work in a factory or an office or anywhere doing repetitive things with your hands (like working on an assembly line, typing, filing or playing the piano) then your hands, wrists, arms and shoulders might start to hurt like hell because they are being overworked. If you don't go and see a doctor the first time you feel twinges, you could be seriously up the creek unable to paddle because it hurts so much.

Having RSI means having to say 'Could you open the lid?' five thousand times a day, always taking the passive role in sex ('Are

you having a good time, dear? Sorry I can't touch you.') and not being able to work. It's vile. At the first sign of it, stop work, and see a doctor and a union representative.

Now, if after all that you're still keen on getting a job and you don't have one, it would be sensible to follow all the usual advice like getting someone to check for spelling mistakes in your job application, not wearing a wetsuit to the interview and remaining determined, happy, committed and optimistic throughout any extended periods of unemployment. Nobody really expects you to accomplish the latter. If you still have the energy, try everything you can think of. Write to your local member of parliament, especially if you live in a marginal electorate. In fact, if you think it will help, chain yourself to his or her front door. At least it will make for a more interesting afternoon.

One situation likely to come up in the course of trying to get a job or actually being in one is sexual harassment, which can range from men staring at your chest, saying sleazy things or trying to feel you

HERMOINE the MODERN GIRL auditions for a rock VIDEO

stand in the corner & moisten your lips, honey.

I beg your pardon, turkey

Oh really. Haven't you got a red leather mini-skirt?

I sense a Duran Duran involvement here...

up in the lift (or elsewhere). The Modern Girl's simple five step guide to combat sexual harassment is as follows:

- Tell the culprit his intentions are not wanted.
- Tape his conversation (optional).
- Report him to your union in confidence and follow their advice.
- Seduce his wife.
- Take his job.

■ FINANCES

Unless you have pots of money there's not much point in being intimately acquainted with the finer points of negative gearing, rollover funds with a deferred pension annuity and a discounted cash flow analysis, and key investment dividend imputation aggregate yields even if it does mean overcoming the double-taxing of dividends.

There are, however, several important points to absorb about this money game. If you don't have very much, spend it on records and going out and having a good time. Make sure you have enough to pay the rent each week if at all possible. If not, take yourself off for some free community advice from your friendly neighborhood legal centre, welfare department or old mate with a few bob to throw around.

Secondly, if you have more money than you know what to do with, there is little opportunity for empathy, but nevertheless, here's what you should do with it all: don't speculate on share index futures, watch for shonky gold companies, especially any mining companies which change their name to include a buzz-word in their title like 'hi-tech' or 'grooveco', which could indicate they've found nothing but wet sand during their extensive drilling in Glen Waverley or Subiaco.

Any companies that claim a definite cure for AIDS, herpes or pre-menstrual tension should be approached with a sturdy, forty-foot

barge pole. If you have vast amounts of money floating around under the cushions of the couch and in jars under the sink, think about backing a strong little Aussie company, and if you're feeling less than benevolent towards the local economy, bung it 'offshore'. This means buying some dinky little units in Japan or investing in an American trust fund.

Management trusts with a good reputation are generally fairly decent things to throw your money at if you've spoken to the sort of stockbroker who can look you in the eye, has a certificate of some sort and doesn't wear a revolving bow-tie.

Luxury cars are an investment, although, personally, I think many girls would do better to drive a stylish two-tone pink 1957 Morris Minor. At least then when you hit a tree you can mourn the loss of perfect duco and not worry where your next meal is coming from. There's no point trying to buy art. Holmes a Court and that Bond person with the beer and boats have been throwing blank cheques around galleries for too long and have inflated the market. If the Australian dollar is plummetting towards new depths, give up going overseas.

Drug-running may be profitable, but risky and probably highly immoral. Besides, you might get shot. Tourist and export industries are the go, and if you have any entrepreneurship coursing through those girlish veins, find a fabulous new invention that will revolutionize something and invest in it. At least you can say you were in a revolution once, which will get you a free cup of coffee in Fitzroy or Glebe when you're down and out one day.

'What about the people who work in the business community?' I hear you ask. Oh, purely out of interest, not that anyone's looking

for a rich person to latch on to. Here it is in a nutshell: stockbrokers sell little bits of companies at a time, merchant bankers mind other people's money, bankers mind other people's money but don't get paid as much, analysts brood a lot, actuaries are people who wanted to be accountants but didn't have the personality, who work out your insurance premiums based on how long they think you'll live (a cheerful lot) and there are also trouble shooters, head-hunters and collectors.

POLITICS

A tricky one, this. Keeping up with the Australian Labor Party these days is a bit like going on a strange military march — you know: left, right, left, right, right, right, right. There is also a mythical 'New Right' which is really just the old right-wing turkeys recruiting new bugs: in fact the New Right is just the Old Right with pimples. Even

more charming as you can well imagine. This shuffle to the right is also supplemented by a disconcerting trend (almost as disturbing as the rumour that flares are coming back) that it is cool to have no opinions on politics.

Ha! Everyone should have opinions, but regard most areas of politics with a decent level of healthy scepticism. Real Modern Girls steer clear of Young Liberals' Mah Jong evenings unless they're going to get free cocktails out of them, and refuse to flirt with nuclear scientists.

It is extremely tempting to view the French Government's nuclear testing in the Pacific with the same abhorrence previously reserved for cellulite, another Gallic phrase foisted into our language along with 'limpet bomb' and 'your uranium is safe with us'. The current debate about whether it is fashionable to be anti-nuclear is going to be a trifle irrelevant if we all get blown up so if you feel like protesting about nuclear weapons, do it with accustomed gusto.

Members of the New/Old Right will try and impress upon you the

importance of cutting welfare benefits for single mothers, shipping Aborigines to Omsk and buying more weapons for their global sandpit. Don't listen: most of them had very bad experiences in the playground at kindy and have been incurably grumpy ever since, poor dears. And the rest are rich and see no reason to run the world any differently, thank you very much. As for personal politics, the following will not be tolerated: sexism, condescension and luke-warm gin.

■ FEMINISM

'I'm not a feminist,' some women say sternly, as they march off to work where Equal Opportunity legislation protects them; as they refuse to do all the housework on the grounds that their husband is perfectly capable, and as they decline to be treated like a small deposit of seagull pooh on the windscreen of life. Rubbish. Women who say they are not feminists and act like individuals with basic human rights have just got their terminology wrong.

Somehow some of us have absorbed the absurd idea that feminism means giving up the following: being funny, wearing skirts and make-up, and heterosexuality. Dear oh dear, they should be told that that's an Old Husband's Tale, and to stop giving feminism a bad name.

Feminism doesn't mean reading every book on the subject of the patriarchy and pornography and equal pay and rape and oppression and the way women have been forced to take up the largest share of poverty. But if you fancy the idea of some research, it might help to understand why we need it.

It's easy for some to look back now and laugh at women who burned their bras and stormed Playboy bunny clubs and jumped up and down until somebody took notice. But if it wasn't for them, there wouldn't be nearly as many women professors and doctors and mechanics and logging engineers and plumbers and stand-up comedians and union officials and chefs and artists and clerks and secretaries.

If you really want all the women in margarine ads to run around looking like mindless berks intent on being congratulated for the perfect seven-course dinner every night of their lives, and you seriously believe women have nothing to give the workforce than a bit of colour and movement, and you don't think women who have chosen to stay at home to look after their kids have a right to some respect and a share of the welfare budget if they need it because their husband never existed or ran away to Venezuela, only then will it become clear that you probably are not a feminist.

Not every feminist is a radical lesbian, although some of those are jolly nice girls, too. There's room for nearly everyone in the feminist boat. I once asked my mum, who was a 'homemaker' for fifteen years, whether she was a feminist. She was absolutely horrified.

HERMOINE and her MUM

You haven't changed since 1964 and suddenly you're fashionable again!

retro paisley

¿sigh¿

Have you been reading 'Dolly' again? Heaven knows I tried to bring you up feminist...

yoga pozzie

'A feminist?' she shrieked. 'Of course I'm a feminist!'

I wasn't, when I was a teenager. I thought mothers should just do all those things for you that dads didn't have to. Then I thought about what I wanted to do when I grew up, and it didn't have a lot to do with staying home for forty years.

Thankfully there were some Modern Girls before my time who fought for a few more opportunities for me, and the rest of us. Some were the first feminists, the suffragettes who sensibly dressed themselves in purple, a very fetching shade, and went out and won the right to vote in some countries. Some of them even went on hunger strikes or threw themselves under horses (probably at the very sight of the stirrups, which reminded them of childbirth).

Others fought, and are still fighting for equal pay, child care, rape crisis centres, family planning clinics, an end to violent pornography and a right to feel cute even if you don't look like an airbrushed peroxide blonde with a figure like a Barbie doll and as many brains as the creatures in the centre pages of one of those men's magazines with the *astoundingly* informative articles.

Just because you don't shave your armpits doesn't mean you hate men. (A man I met at a country music festival once disagreed with me on this point, truly.) We need men, even ones who blow their nose in the shower, because they give us the means to give birth to more feminists, and then we can take over the wor . . . sorry, got a bit carried away. I think we all recognize that some men can be really thoroughly decent fellows and you'll find most of the rest listed under 'Men To Steer Clear Of'.

Sometimes us feminists are given a hard time by people who accuse us of all sorts of things, like despising motherhood, and lacking a sense of humour, and taking the jobs of young men who could be working if we'd just go away and iron someone's shirts. Do not under any circumstances react to this sort of criticism by yelling, spitting, shaving your head or doing anything else to confirm their stereotype. Laugh. Remind them, with a tolerant smile on your face, that you quite agree that some women would be better off ironing shirts for a living, starting with Margaret Thatcher and Nancy Reagan.

LIFE IN GENERAL OR PHILOSOPHY

Everyone's got a theory on how to run your life. If it's not the Mormons beetling through your front gate on rickety bicycles with a clear intention of praying in the loungeroom while 'Countdown' is on, it's your horoscope in the *Sun-Herald* warning you that times may be tough but to keep a clear head. Not altogether helpful, really. Advice comes from such diverse sources as women's magazines, American pop psychologists with polystyrene teeth and

nylon hair, Tarot cards, dietary experts, charismatic tram conductors, game show hosts, fortune cookies, tea leaves, tea ladies and T-shirts. What can a Modern Girl rely on these days?

■ THINGS NOT TO TRUST

- Chemical companies and nuclear power
- Most forms of contraception
- Advertising
- Men who ask 'What do women really want?' (Sometimes it's a lasting relationship, sometimes it's a chocolate icecream.)
- Love at first sight

■ THINGS YOU SHOULD TRUST

- Instinct
- Most mums
- Big brothers
- Best friends
- Lust at first sight

Perhaps it is too much to ask to have a motto for life but something my Dad always told me as a young child probably still holds true: 'If you can't laugh, you're fucked.'